I

First Printing: 2020
ISBN 978-1-79484-578-7

SHOCKORAMA BOOKS INC.
4425 South Mopac Expressway.
STE 601
AUSTIN, TX. • 78735

This type in this book is set in Athelas Regular and Italic.

www.BobSchneider.com

NIGHTINGALES

BOB SCHNEIDER

Shockorama Books

What Me Worry?

They live on fish
They wear pants
They walk upright
They sing the old
Songs in their native
Tongue occasionally
They hunt the wolf into extinction
They curtain off their bedrooms
They line their mausoleums
With the skulls of their enemies
They drink the Kool aid when
The man says to drink up
They offer up their children
To an unseen god
They rope off a section
Of the club to keep the riff raff out
They figure out how
To make t-shirts out of bamboo
And old aluminum cans
They toil in relative obscurity
Their entire lives and are grateful
For the opportunity to do so
They gather in large groups
To feel safe or powerful
I'm not sure which, because I'm not one of them
All of the things that make them comfortable
Usually freak me out
I'm just glad there are laws to keep
Them from hurting me
They roll their own cigarettes
They buy their cigarettes pre-rolled
They operate heavy machinery
They wear lacy underwear
They go without wearing underwear

They sink to the bottom of the
Ocean after they've been dragged
Overboard by an icy crab cage
At first, they're surprised and angry
But as all hope is lost, they resign
Themselves to their fate
They play games involving inflatables
They dress in uniforms and kill
Each other in remote locations
They've been sent to by men
Who are just doing their duties
The duties that men have to honor
They fight for their flag and country
Their school and god almighty
They read books written hundreds of years
Ago and believe them to be true
Even today when so much of
What was written so long ago
Is clearly fabricated or at best
An exaggeration of events
They may or may not have occurred
They lie in bed at night
And listen for noises in the darkness
There shouldn't be any noises
Because they're alone in the house
And they're relieved when indeed
They don't hear anything, but then
There is a sound. Did they just
Imagine it or did something shift
It must have been the wind
Blowing something over outside
They lie down in the road
And stop the tanks from proceeding
Any further and then are never
Heard from again and the next time
The tank is rolling down the promenade,
It does so unencumbered and with

Military ease and precision
They drive through the night
Listening to songs sung by dead
People who lived thirty or forty years
Ago, but sound like they are as alive as KISS II
Right there in the car with you. But they're not.
They look at photos of insects
And realize that every photograph
Of an insect, is the photograph
Of a dead insect, just like
Every photograph of every
Person every taken will soon
Be the photograph of a dead person
Every airport is named after a ghost
Every library is filled with the books
Of the dead. I'm eating something
That is dead as I write this
When you are eating something
That was once alive it's important
To know when that thing died
They build vast underground cities
And live in the ocean and breathe
Fire and call themselves friends of
The poor, but the poor have no friends.
They've closed off part of the freeway
Making it almost impossible to get
To where you are going on time
They stick their noses in other people's
Business. They own businesses and
Work for people that have businesses
And burn businesses to the ground
To collect on the insurance and sometimes
Go to jail because they are caught
Because they are so fucking stupid
And obviously haven't watched as
Much Investigation Discovery Network
Television as my wife has

They lock and load
They bundle up
They make nice
They hurt the ones they love
They keep indoors
They live outside the norm
They spy with their eyes
Something of a particular hue
And ask the people around
Them to guess what that particular
Object might be
They pile on
They smear the queer
They measure twice and cut once
They hang themselves in their
Apartment from the bedroom door
Using a belt because the medication
Stopped working and what's the point, I mean
It's not going to get any better
And no one cares and it's all
Going to end soon anyway.
They run out of ideas
They run for office
They run the show
They run down to the store
They run off with the Baker's boy
They climb out of the hole
They've been stranded in for
Over three months defying
All the odds and they can't even speak
A word of English.
They usually make better decisions as they get
older
They hole up
They break down at the office, but very rarely
Most of the time they just show up and do their

Job and then go home and try to forget what just
happened
They wear white shirts
And red dresses and
Cowboy boots and wedding rings
And halter tops and mood pendants
And hair extensions and rub creams
And balms into the folds of their skin
They tackle the hard problems
They shift their positions on complex issues
They learn to let go and let god
They love a good mystery
They yearn for home when they are far
Away from home and have lost their
Way and are probably never going
To get back home again.
They cry when the music plays
In the background when the lovers
Finally embrace as the snow falls
Past the balcony and onto the fingerless
Homeless forgotten losers lying in the streets
Below

The Great Flood

The time, when the world
On its head was ending
You took my hand and
We ran through the night

But only in my head
I was dry as a hand bone
The only rain falling
Outside on the lawn

And the world
Wasn't ending
At all

Things In Boxes

We all live in
A yellow submarine
Yellow submarine
Yellow submarine

We all live in a
Yellow submarine
In the middle of the
Ocean

Surrounded by monsters

Mike Tyson Vs. The Kool Aid Man™

These pictures of our kids
When they were younger.
Pictures of ourselves when we were kids
Looking into the camera with our mouths open.

The world piling onto our shoulders
One day at a time. Until we can barely stand.
Putting out the fire with Girl Scout cookies.

Acquitted,

That's how I feel now
Wearing the clothes of an older man
Buying underwear in packs of three
Sometimes four

I smile at people. Not because I feel like smiling
It's so they won't feel uncomfortable around me
So they'll tell others how nice I am

I mean, I'm nice, but
I don't smile around the house
I'm not smiling right now as I write this.
I'm staring off into the light, dying

It's So Much Harder To Be Stupid When
You're So Much Smarter Than Someone Who
Is Really Dumb

Putting the dishes away
After smashing them into
All the stars in heaven

Cleaning the blood out of the rug
Unfolding the laundry
Dreaming of a better president
Separating out the good animals
In the forest from the bad ones

Bending a knee and then
Breaking a knee.
Folding a knee into a triangle
And giving it to the widow
Of a dead soldier

Finding a knee on your lawn
Calling the cops immediately and
Finding out in the most dramatic fashion
That it's your own knee!

Now you have an extra knee
When it comes to knees, it's finders' keepers
You donate the knee to the election committee
They ask you if you have any more knees
You tell them you do, and donate all your knees

You start an orphanage for knees
Now you have more knees than you
Know what to do with

In an article in Buzzfeed a small child
Is lost and the whole town goes out into the woods
At night in their pajamas looking for it
And all they find are knees

Your Version Vs. Mine
(I Guess)

What the spotted owl is to the
Oil stains in the driveway

What the career ending suicide
Is to a sideways glance

What 'Been there, Done that'
Is to 'Wash and Wear'

What two hundred dollars is
To a left-hand turn

What Miley Cyrus is to
A flea circus in France

What a 'make out sess' is to
Falling down a flight of stairs

What dead men's wishes are to
The great Russian forest

What the heart of the great blue whale is
To a Volkswagen bug

What a pancreatic tumor is
To a dying field of roses

Simple Math

Divide the ocean by four.
Subtract last week's dinner
At your parent's house.

Multiply that by
This persistent pain
In my left knee.

Take into account the three years
I can't get back in El Paso and
Take out the part where the car got towed

Then you might start to get an idea
Of where everything began
To just 'go right'

Facing The Sun

Earlier this morning
I was running down the street
Pulling rainbows out my feet
Flames covering all your kisses

A psychedelic magician
Holding a dead baby.
But it wasn't a dead baby
It was only a little girl. Alive and

Laughing. Commanding me
To give her a piggyback ride
The world not as bad as it seems
To be, all the time

Stand Up

There's very little
That hasn't been
Picked through
In the light

To happen upon the few
Great undiscovered treasures
You must go into
The great darkness

Someone Behind Me

An alligator
Crawling across
Your kitchen floor
Pretending to be

A human being
Dressed in a suit and tie
Carrying important papers
Pretending to be

The last seven hours where you
Were imagining lights in the sky
Above your house, perhaps
From another world,

Coming down, out
Of the sky, to
Scoop you up
And save you

Somehow

The Newest Season Of The Bachelor

Repeating the names of all seven angels
He walks the perimeter of town
Spiking the ball in the end zone
The crowd chanting his name

Earlier in the evening he
Put the final touches
On a beautiful bouquet of flowers
He'd decided to give to the president

He rushes to the post office
But it is burned to the ground
And so is most of the town

Sifting through the bodies he comes across
An old telephone number and without hesitation
Dials it.

The voice on the other line a stranger now,
Years older. Teeth bent back out of shape

Why have you waited till now to call?
Well, it's only now that I came across your
number

He puts the phone down and swims across the sea
To America where the world is ending

He builds an army of space robots
But they aren't really space robots

Just piles of shit he's
Made in his small apartment
Over the course of a few months

The police have been notified and
No one's watching The Bachelor™ tonight

They've all laid down their swords and decided
Tonight, enough is enough

Just A Little Faster Please

I became best friends with Bob Dylan
It happened quite naturally
Last summer as the world was ending

Hiding inside the mountains
Down to our last two cans of beer
Breathing in the black dust
The sky had become

Tearing apart the beautiful rags of the past
And passing them back and forth
Between us

Through The Tweaks

This sun's light speaks
In its ancient language
Disguising the truth
With magnificent lies

The Only Life You Could Save Was The Life
Of The Dude Getting High On Skittle Brand
Giraffe Milk

There's a show my wife watches called
The Real Housewives Of Beverly Hills.
I watched some of it with her last night.

One woman wore a costume
That gave away the ending
To just about every movie ever made.

Her face so smooth
You could almost see the reflection
Of a more beautiful world

Every once in a while, the show
Was interrupted by short little movies.
About people just like you and me:

Actors? Yes, but also people,
With problems. Real problems
Like soft penises and poisoned blood

The inability to control their own legs
Things I didn't even know you could get
But people did, I assume

Each little movie always ended the same way
With the narrator describing the terrible side
effects of these preventative medications

On screen the actors delighted in fun activities
I assume this was an artistic decision
Made by the director

Still, I could hardly wait to get back
To the main show and the smooth skin and
transfigured bodies

Of what I can only assume were monsters or
Demons that had taken over these housewives, in
Southern California

Later that night, after taking my third dose
Of Tenormin™, I finally decided to kill myself
And that felt like the right thing to do

Another Beautiful Day On The Bus

The world hasn't ended
Like you thought it might
Everything's not gone forever
But it's easy to imagine death's

Long beautiful fingers
Stroking your soft little head
Caressing you to sleep in the back of the limo
Giving you the coldest kisses ever

Rooms I've Never Seen

My hand doesn't
Hurt anymore
Because it's on
Your arm

Holding another hand
Which isn't my hand because
It belongs to the body of Christ
Who is in heaven

With my arms
And my haircut
The best one yet
A model cut

Diamonds cover
Every strand
Reflecting the light
Like a piano

That can only be
Played by someone else
Never touched
Only spoken of

In dreams

Space Man

It's OK
Waiting for forever
Just don't forget
To turn off the stove

It's Hard To Write A Good Song These Days

My mind was once full of music
And melodies and ideas
Now it's a forest of facts
And figures and formulas
I can still remember what it was
Once like...well, sort of
It's only a memory
A city that floats out
Onto the ocean
And is gone
But not quite
Forgotten

Lazarus

I removed my wet things
And laid them out
On your kitchen table
The sunlight streaming
Through the window

I had been swimming in
Two lakes at the same time,
But in different clothes
One made my lies bigger
The other, my life easier

Lessons 35-72

I begged for you to take me
Far away to the country after working
For years as a janitor in relative obscurity
But you did not come

I turned into a mountain drive
Locking myself in a stolen car
Listening to Air Supply
Searching for small jewels
But you did not come

I walked over to your apartment
After taking acid in college and
Watched the movie about the girl
Who had turned herself into a bird
Lying about what I was feeling
Because I couldn't understand it at the time
But you still didn't come

I wrote you a letter
Using perfume instead of blood
Leaving the front door open
Every night for a year and still,
You did not come

And before any of this
I was alone and asked you
If you might be able to save
Me from any or all of it but
The outcome remained the same

Something Rich And Strange

I coughed up something
That looked like a wave
On the face of the sea
From a great distance

The moon perhaps
Or a space above
The ceiling of an
Airplane

Becoming the proud father
Of a baby praying mantis
It had my eyes
And its mother's mouth

Each raindrop adorned
With a small noose
Something to cling to
While your life flew past

The Other One

Without a shirt
I move through the crowd
Like a swimming pool

A cowboy now
With my ruined hair
And broken back

Writing this love
Letter using a crayon
Drawing a rainbow

With the one color
You had left me
Blue

Out To The Edge

I ate the red beans
The ones with the faces on them
Out by Description Pass

Where they've hauled in lots
Of bodies from that lake
Men, women and children

I saw a ghost there
Once, plain as day
White as wonder

Whatever And Ever

You put the book away
Thinking you'll never
Write anything this good

Studying the author's photo
You come to the realization
That even if you were her equal

And everyone loved you for your work
Most of the world
Would never know your name

And the few that did would
Eventually die and you
Would still be lost forever

Like everyone else that came before
And even if that wasn't true
It wouldn't matter

Anyway

Flesh & Blood

In this scene

The monk is combing
King Kong's beard

Both of them,
Enjoying the view

King Kong, longing
For the anonymous days

His hands the size
Of Volkswagens

Tender as tangerines
Boneless, so they hover

Just above the water
Where fish sleep

Dreaming of flies

How Michelle Obama Got Her Groove Back

We hid our old bodies
Inside these new ones
Wearing our disguises
Inside out

Walking through town
Like nothing had changed
With sunglasses on
Our conversation taking us

Back in time
Away from the flames
Where the ashes we wore
Became clothes again

The rooms of our lives
Filled with the money
Stolen from the hotel room
While we were away

Things To Do:

1. Buy something

2. Find a spot nearby and lay in it

4. Develop a Canadian Christmas band

5. Eat more expensive cheese

7. Go to the bathroom soon

8. Grow misty-eyed looking out over the great grey fields of western Texas

9. Really finally get started on learning how to do a great 'deaf guy' impression

10. When swearing the oath, tell nothing but lies, lies, lies

11. Drive around the neighborhood in the middle of the afternoon wondering what these people are like that live in these houses. What are their lives like? What do they do when they're alone? Oh, the humanity!

14. Be not young and continue growing older

18. Warm up the ham that's in the fridge or throw it out or do something with it for Christ's sake

24. Start writing better poems

Anniversary

A monster
Walks into a room
With some really
Beautiful pants on

Breathing it all in
I lay by the pool
With my head just
Below the surface

So I can't hear what
You're saying.
You'll need to speak
Louder and say everything

You've ever lied to me about
Again and again, again

You Don't Become A Billionaire
By Telling Strangers Your Secrets

I love accents
The way they roll
Around your mouth
And fill your head
With ice crystals
Diamond clouds
Louder mountains

Once I was
The iciest king
Of forever
Freezing your
Face with my
Grape teeth

I'd bake your cake
On a yellow river
Inside your
Feeling longer

Across
The street
Is who I used
To be
Before I
Became
This

Tina Turner

All the black girls
At my house
Were lying on the floor
Taking out their underwear
And wrapping them around
The moon

I threw my phone
Into the ocean
And tore my clothes off
Catching all the rays

I've been
Peeing the entire
Time I've been writing this
Into my pants
And all over
The floor

We Dem Boys

Watching the television
Dreaming of the better world
I woke up in the white house
The sheets smelling
Of sandalwood

A vampire bat hanging from the ceiling
The presidential seal on the carpeting
My legs shaking I could hardly walk
I called down for a sandwich
And a bottle of Coke

The spiders laying their eggs
In my ears

They brought it to my room immediately
The secret service man's penis
Clearly visible in the golden light of the hallway
Blood pouring through
And into my eyes

Taking Off Our Masks

I found a splinter in my spine
Oh how it glowed
And shined the tiniest thing
I ever know'd

A little tree
In the shape of a mole
A little girl
With a fishing pole

And suddenly the
Sound of planes
But not planes
Something more like

Rain filling the sky
With shadows
Tall and thin and then
Nothing at all

Hansel

Old witch with your bruised hands
And wild talk and strange sense of humor
Your long shadow
Even at night

Leaning against the door
Begging me for a bite
With your bad breath
And poor eyesight

Asking me to stick
My thumb through the grate
Me in my torn nylons
Holding out a chicken bone

At The End Of The Sea

Fingers of wind
Made of birds
Most of the city
Is dreaming

The depths of
Your mouth
Teeming with
Words

Ghosts
Mostly
Thirsty and
Gleaming

Bob Dylan Looking Into Someone's Window
(In The Rain)

My mouth is
Black as cake
Until I speak
Then diamonds

Cover everything

I often wonder
If everything were different
Would everything still
Be the same?

Parts Unknown

In a room lined with blue rocks
While your children were dreaming
And every door thrown open

Birds flew through the air
Their mouths full of feathers
Singing as loud as they could

The song you had written about the
Camel that wouldn't carry another day
Not even the tiniest piece of straw

Looping the belt around your neck
Closing it in the door
Making the decision there'd be

No more bedtime stories
Just goodbye kisses
And could've beens

All The Ladies Love You

Where you lived, no matter how blue the sky was
Or how bright green the fields burned
All summer long

If it was time to get up and out of bed
And dig a grave. You'd get up and out of bed
And dig a grave

And when the Mexicans congregated
In the discotheques, late at night and
You couldn't remember where the gold was
buried

It didn't stop you from going out as well
You knew, if you had a song, you'd be okay
And even if you didn't, you knew you'd get one
before too long

Because words come easy to a broken heart
They come easy when you are falling apart

And when you died, and they marked your grave
With the words of your choice
The vampires came out that night
And danced among the stones

And your mother held you
In her arms as you died by the sea
Whispering softly in your ear
"All the ladies love you

All the ladies love you
My sweet beautiful boy"

58

Dear "Santa"

The halls of the dead
Are filled with corpses
Oh, how they love to dance

Their skin glowing in the grey
Their bones falling out behind
Them along the path of forever

Forgetting their cares and worries
Lighting expensive pipes
Exhaling black confetti

Stamping their boots
Against the ceiling of heaven
The dirty years behind them

Their buttonholes sewn shut
Their coats wrapped around the
Planets of their hearts

Their rainbows glowing
Like giant snakes
Across the sky

El Negro

I'm singing my song
In Spanish

The way it was intended to be sung
In a high falsetto

The girls in the back of the room
Their dresses half hanging off their shoulder

Smoking cigarillos
Calling out my name

In Spanish
The sparks flying off their faces

Their mouths open
As if to catch a fly

Nightingales

You showed up
To the dance
In the dream
Without shoes
Without a chance

Alone forever

We danced
Like two potatoes
With toothpick arms
On the rim of the moon
Cloudless

Guns and Ammo

I'm writing the grand poems
The ones that change the world

They're so hard to write
Every line must be as bulletproof as

The promising presidential candidate's
Outdoor parade route

The day after
His anti-gun legislation speech

Everybody Died

Everybody died
My mom and dad
My kids. my friends

One world at a time

Everyone I'd ever met
Or read about
Every single person

Died. Even me

Do You Ever Wonder

I live on this planet
In outer space

Every night I sit at my desk
In a small room that faces the jungle

My ears are covered in a thick fur
Small black dots cover my neck and jaw

My wife is looking
Through my phone on our bed

I've noticed large ants
Gathering in the room

A spider is laying its eggs
Near the television where

Abe Zapruder holds a Zoomatic
Director Series camera in his hands

While the president is escorted into
Heaven by the most beautiful angels

I have ever seen

The Cosby Show

The ghost of you
From before
Leads us down
The heart of the freeway

Cars piling up outside
Your window
You should be able
To see yourself by now?

In the clown suit you paid
For with my money, man!
The cops
Circling your houses

Halcyon

The night turning
On its black hinges

The white light
Of your kisses
In the doorway
Of your old house

Those days
And the rest

Lost little snakes
Snapping at your
Ankles

As the sun rises
To uncover another
Glorious day

Don't Wake The Bear

Make the call
To your boyfriend
In Portugal secretly

The teeth in your
Face yellowing
Your feet flattening

A car parked
A block from your house
A stranger inside

"No officer, we didn't
See any of it coming.
Everything seemed normal"

The dog barking
In the backyard
For no reason

A noise from the other
Room and then
Silence

Sharp Enough

I became thinner than air
So thin I could see through

The door of your apartment
So thin I couldn't move

At first but then the drugs
Wore off and I found myself

On a train in Switzerland
Riding through the world

As thin as a spider's web
Catching everything

That came across my
Thin path

West Point

In the parking lot
Outside your apartment
Your bed is burning

The smoke lifting up
The black night's skirt
Curling around

The moons white lashes

The beat breaks
The world in half
And out spill the stars

Chappaquiddick

It would be so much easier
To write these poems
If I was just a little smarter,
Could put a sentence together better,
And wasn't so tired all the time

Oh, I don't let that stop me, though
I can do whatever I want, see

Write the stupidest poems ever
Talk about my nuts, I mean
Really get into talking about my nuts
And the way they greet the queen
When she visits the house early in the spring

The only woman on earth

The way my nuts block out the sun
As she lies naked by the pool
Her pussy...her old grey wrinkled pussy
On display in the shadows of my
Immense hairy nut sack

Stop All That Crying

I had a great idea for a poem
This morning, but

Now I can't recall what it was
And all I can write about

Is not remembering

I thought that might be cool
When I started

I thought maybe
I'd remember what it was

I never did. These ideas only
Come around once

Cars speeding past a dusty old gas station
My mind, an old man with his head on crooked

Legs sore from a overused life
A mouth full of birds

And coffee

Kansas

The way the world
Sort of slanted a bit and never
Really went back to the way it was
Ever again, and of course me,
Using this corrective
Stance ever since
Off balance, but
Not enough to
Notice really

The Smudge Of Newsprint

Bringing the hammer down
Onto his thumb and through the table
Into the ground and past the earth's crust
Down into hell where the devil is making
Breakfast for his little baby girl
The birds of death flying overhead
Their red feathers falling into the
Frying pan while his imaginary wife
Calmly reads the paper

Planet Of The Apes

Taking your audience
Into consideration
Is the death of art

Writing for people
Without a sense of humor
And no imagination
Is the end of anything
Interesting to say

Concern for the reader
Who takes everything personally
And can't understand that you
Are trapped inside yourself

With nowhere to go but out
And you're so scared it hurts,
Means the devil is winning,
And the world has lost

Fat People Eating McDonald's At The Airport

I have no interest in
Telling you my opinion
Of things that I've noticed
People doing

I love the poets who do, though
I prefer to exaggerate
Or completely fabricate
Everything

For instance,
I saw all these fat people
Eating McDonald's at
The airport

Michigan

He collected scissors
Just a few hundred at first, then thousands.
He filled the house of his first wife with them
Then the houses of his mistresses

He bought a building in downtown
Detroit and raised a family there
At night you could hear them
Singing inside the stone walls

His back to the speaker
Lost in the shuffle
Leaving all that was lost
To what little was left

God (One Of The Good Guys)

God was hiding in a coconut tree
And the little Indians
That ran around underneath
Making their butter
Hooting and hollering
Never suspected a thing

They would sing in
Their native tongue of
The Water Spirit or the
Great Interloper who would ride
Though the land on
A painted pony

God would listen
Enjoying the sweet
Nut water and chuckle to himself
Amused by these lovely fools
He had created with their
Wild thoughts and wonderful hairdo's

And he loved them
Even the more with
Each passing day
And every far fetched
tale of spirits and gods
And science and other
Such wonderful nonsense

Da Bears

The big pink
'I love you a lot' bear
And the 'I'm sick of your shit' bear
Took turns being

Good ol' bears

Conversing about
Work and laughing
At stupid jokes
Licking the drying blood
From their sticky paws

The World Around Our Heads

Your rough hands
Covered in ashes
Inside those older
Skinnier jeans

Telling me the story
Of the time you went
To North Dakota and
Shot someone in the face

And how afterwards
You'd lie in bed at
Night knowing exactly
How empty

This world
Really is

Minister Of Drugs

Take your car
And the car in front of you
And turn them into
One real crazy super car
And you get
To see god

A lumpy little loaf
Steam coming off it
All the brilliant reds
Of the world
Together at last
The nightly news
You're on it pumpkin

Every Green Moment

When the storm came
Unexpectedly, and all I could
Think about were the deer

After your mom died
And I was sure she was
In the room with us

After we rebuilt
The car's engine together
In the backyard

Our greasy black fingers
Wrapped around those
Cold coke bottles

The sun beginning
To set over, then back
Behind the barn

Losing itself in the woods
Leaving us with
Nothing but stars

I Thought I Was The Only One

The king walked into the room
On fire and screaming your name.
You took out your teeth and
Proceeded to sing him to sleep

In a version of Spanish
You'd learned in a dream
Where the English bears
(The kindest of all bears)

Were polishing their cruel teeth
And peeking out behind
Their yellow mouths in
The green English morning

Netflix

Today is one of those days
Where it's impossible to imagine monsters
Or write anything special

Where life is a blanket
That folds you into
The couch

Where the TV is something
You are lost inside
Your toes peeking out

Death in
Another county
The coffee getting cold

Stompbox

I love you because
The stars are only inches
From the sea
And yet the whole
World seems
So far away

It seems bigger in the dark
This hole in the sky
Touching the trees
With it's sad silver face

I love you because
When you
Hold me
Sometimes
I don't feel
A thing

How Music Works

You stop pretending
You're good friends with David Byrne
And start to believe it

You ask him
When you'll be getting
Together again?

You both laugh
Because you know how busy
You both are.

He's telling you
About the concert he put together
Back in the early two thousands

You're not feeling lonely at all now
You stop reading and just sit there all alone
Talking to David Byrne in

Your head while the world
Swings through space
And your life

Goes swooshing
Off into
Forever

It's Hard To Say What It All Means, Really

Throwing the couch
Off the roof

Putting his hand
Through the engine block

The black beacon
Of despair

The empty house
Once filled with children

The shadows of trees
Hidden in the forest

And the end of
All our dreams

Big Hands

He got them big hands
That brings them birds
Back from the dead

Makes 'em sing again
The songs of the dead
They swing in his hair at night

Like old men, setting his face on fire
The tears streaming down
His cheeks in wonder

Star Smoke

You bow down before
The Lord shivering and afraid
And full of shame

A thin towel wrapped
Around your legs
Birds living in your beard

You remember all the
Words of every song
You've ever sung

You smile
And it is the only
Time you've ever smiled

Your face
Falls to the floor
With a clang

Waking the stranger
Sleeping beside you
In the car

You have a meeting
In a coffee shop in Seattle
Concerning a musical event

It will never take place
The woman you're talking to
Occasionally writing

Down notes with an
Orange Crayola marker

All hope lost

You grow much older
And die one afternoon
In a hospital bed

Your son, his heart breaking
Allowing the nurse to discontinue
The life support

The world
Spinning through
Space forever

Clouds of galaxies
Gathering together
At the edges

That's Just The Rain

The difference between a few wrinkles
And a few more wrinkles is the difference
Between you being left to die alone on the street
And the president calling and coming
Over with some sandwiches he* made

*Please note the use of the masculine pronoun
When referring to the president*

Old men fill hotels with
Young girls every night and have been
Since there were old men and hotels

Money and power are the only
Weapons you have against time
And we men are pretty stingy with those

The Tree

I am tree
My face and feet are tree
My penis are tree
My organs are tree
They only appear
In this poem

My dreams are tree
Hauled across the world
On the beds of trucks
Driven by men who
Leave their homes
In the morning and return
Later (often alone)

People pretend to be nice
(and sometimes aren't pretending)

I used to hang out with the son
Of the guy who started Blockbuster video
He sold his company at just the right time

I used to own so many CD's I didn't know
What to do with them all

I was tree then
Because I have always been tree
And these words
On this thin piece of tree
Waiting to be read

The American War

The presidential race
Lasted most of the weekend

We celebrated our
Victory aboard the
USS Enterprise

The whole crew was there
Lt. Uhura in her yellow uniform
Handing out the "punch cards"

I was unable to approach her
And left before the police showed up

As I was leaving I saw Captain Kirk weeping
He had been struggling with depression
The ship speeding through endless space

Inside the paramount pictures movie building
The useless lights of the ship's control system
Blurred and blinking in the background

The Cincinnati Slant

Tying your shirt
Across your front teeth

The eyeteeth

You take your seat
Inside the stadium

It's so loud, you can hardly see
You reach for something
It might be a penis
Or a cell phone
(the ear bone of a whale perhaps)
The disappointment of a lover

You see small campfires
In the distance

Your soft fists are making
Circles in the air
You realize you are part of
Something much larger
A wave or perhaps

The ocean

You reach your arms
Into the black universe
And sit back down
The adrenalin
Working its way
Through your body
Your lover's disappointment
Forgotten

Sometimes It's Good To See

Your name might as
Well be a bowling
Alley in my mouth

Breaking my teeth
Off into the gutter
Little skydivers

Their small hands
Cupping the holy water
Fish swimming in their depths

Wearing the boots of beggars
Filled with thorns

Starburst wrappers
Cover the living room

While bombs explode
In the background

The naked reporter on CNN
Dipping her cheeseburger
Into the BBQ sauce

Quietly telling me
'She's loving it'

Her thin hipbones exposed
She can't be more than thirty
Death a distant dream

Stay Till The End

Falling through
A wall
30 stories
Above your legs

Monkey mouth
Making out
In a dark cloud
Of kisses

In Italian
Your face
Looks like
A swastika

Everything's Oklahoma

I laid my head
On the yellow pillow
At the party

With the good weed
After meeting the Butthole
Surfers' Manager

Who had just made the
Freshest blotter
I took it and

Moved into the future
With the new knowledge
That there was more

Than one way to experience
Everything and nothing
Was ever the same

Again

CIA Bag Drop

Put the B in the oven
Close the oven
Fold both doors over your face
Close all the doors

You must pretend

Turn on the oven
Take the B out of the oven
Go to heaven on a little rowboat

That everything
Will never end

Draw a picture of an oven
All the hands of the dead
Form a band called B and
Acquire a ghost's limp

In order to make
It through another day.

In The Nights And Mornings
(April 18, 1955)

I keep writing the world's best poems
It's pretty easy with this golden pen
That the lord gave me years ago
I keep waiting for it to run out of ink
But it just keeps cranking out the hits
One after a-fucking 'nother
It reminds me of this story...

In Other Countries

I hear of the great poet's death
We have become friends somehow
Beyond all expectations

How have I come to this place
It doesn't seem to matter

The last time we spoke
I had been making jokes about
People who had been murdered

He wasn't laughing

Standing before the well
The world closing in around him
Holding his final hand

Poetry Foundation Dot Org
(Can Go And Suck A Dick I Guess)

Critics like to write about poetry
And music and movies and art
They write and write and write
Man, they sound so intelligent
They use words like '_____' and '_____'
That way the reader will be sure of two things:
The critic is qualified and knowledgeable
And will be able to guide us through this darkness

Do we see their poetry? Of course not.
They don't sing and paint or dance
Maybe they are too critical of themselves
Maybe the voices inside them
That they borrowed from their father
Or mother won't allow them to run
And dance and shake for joy
Inside the place that we
All have inside of us
The one below where
Everything comes from.

So

They just write and write in that
Stupid boring voice and feel like
It's the least they can do
And it is

Let's Call It A Life

The younger man looked like he was going to
punch the older man in the face for a second

She looked like she might throw her baby to the
ground momentarily

It looked like the car was coming into our lane

It seemed as if an eternity would pass before she
began to breathe

It looked like the burden of everything would be
too much for her to bear for very much longer

He was looking inside the apartment and saw that
it was empty and she was finally gone

He was staring into the mirror at his parents house
when he realized he had grown old and almost
certainly unlovable

She was looking around for a familiar face and
saw only extras in someone else's movie

He was gazing out across the sea when he began to
see a monster rising out of the depths and up and
into the black clouds of heaven even though there
was nothing to see except the dark and distant
horizon

The Living

Lying on the lake
Her feet hanging
Over the edge

The dead with their
Grave hands reaching up
To her from below

The car doors closing
Outside in the street
Footsteps coming

Up the walkway
Soon it would all be over
And no one would ever

Scare any
Of them
Ever again

Writing A Fantastic Poem At The Airport On Your Phone While Waiting For Your Life To Be Over

There is a demon playing piano
On this guy's t-shirt
Sitting across from me

He keeps making 'important' business calls
And then talking into his laptop
Type, type, typing away

I'm in no hurry
The plane's sitting outside the window
Assed up and ready to go

My next wife won't answer the phone
There's also a guy on TV in a grey t-shirt
And a baseball cap facing backwards

He has a beard, so
I assume he's a full-grown man
Only posing as a small child

The 'newscasters' are discussing
The death of a comedienne who passed away
Unexpectedly last week

All of these people are sitting in front of
microphones
They must have important things to say, I imagine
But the volume is turned down

What am I missing.
So much is happening all the time

All over the world

Crazy stuff!
My friend told me about a boy
Holding up a severed head

He saw in the news recently
I see the boy quite clearly in my mind
He is dressed like Amal from the Christmas play.

He has a karate kid style bandana.
He's a cute kid who you'd normally see playing
baseball or video games.
Sort of a brunette version of my own son.

He's got a gun strapped to his back
He's covered in dust and ashes
He's finally getting the attention he deserves
From these lunatics he is surrounded by

I wonder who's head he's holding?
If it was the head of the comedienne
I wouldn't have to wonder any more

But it's not.

It's just some Middle Eastern stranger
A ghost. A prop. No one to concern myself with
Here in this airport surrounded by animals

The Summer In Jamaica I Spent My Whole Life Living

We plant the seeds that God has given us
Usually at night when wolves
Gather at the corner of the forest
Their eyes catching the reflection
Of our campfires

The screams of the prisoners in the distance

Our skirts embroidered
With the images of the fallen
Singing in a harmony
That has become alien
To my western colleagues

We gather together
Falling to the forest floor
Laughing and remembering
The dreams we had where we
Were flying

The screams of the prisoners in the distance

Buying A Gun

I thought about buying a gun
Then thought about writing a poem
About buying a gun

Then, thought about writing a poem
About thinking about buying a gun
And not buying a gun

Then imagined that
George Harrison wasn't really dead
That he was a monster
And didn't want the world
To see what he'd become

Then imagined,
My best friend was also a monster
With huge hands and black fingernails
His back covered with Fruit loops
And thick matted hair

I imagined he had a
Girlfriend in a wheel chair
But she wasn't a girl
She was a monster as well

I asked myself if I could
Stomach all these monsters?
I thought about my life
And thought, I probably could

I thought about how hard it might be to
Break into a library and steal rare books
Then I wrote this poem

Hands

The hands of Aunt Jemima
Caught half dressed
Grey donuts pounding on the
Bedroom door
At 3 am

The hands of the apocalypse
Pressed hard and
Spreading out over the earth
Like spiders

The hands of the horse
Lying beside you in your dress
The space between the barn
And the backyard stirring
A glass of vermouth

The hands of the vampire
Damp with dew
The morning a vague
Memory from its youth
The blood drying in its mouth

The hands of the former running back
Putting the key into the lock
Of his front door while the sun
Rises like a giant god
From behind the great mountain

The hands of the movie industry
Wrestling the money away
From your teen daughter's
Bank account one Wild Cherry Icee at a time

The hands of Minnesota
Covered in moss and mosquitos
Ten thousand fingers
The color of laughter

The hands of Julie Christie
The second or was it the first wife
Of the famous director
His future wife an unborn baby
At the time of their wedding

The hands of the five comedians
Who swept through town like a wild fire
Burning the theater to the ground
Burning the house next to the theater
To the ground

Remind Me Where I Am Again?

The hard road we were on an hour ago that
Turned into this soft sand beach
In the middle of nowhere
The diapers thrown across the living room
The trash in the garbage disposal
That won't ever work again, until
The guy comes over and fixes it
Showing you the red button that fixes everything

You try the red button on other things
You find that it works like a fucking charm
You use the red button on this train of thought
And BLAM! now you've got this terrific poem

Your chair rises up into heaven
You are the mighty poet king now
Being welcomed there by Jesus and
Hundreds of millions of angels
The air alive with fleas and flying bugs
All the bugs of the world that have ever lived
Alive forever in heaven, with all the animals
And people and fish and everything
That's ever drawn a breath
All smiling and dancing and having sex
And looking better than they have in years

Collision

A bad winter
Parked outside
The Seven-Eleven

The brakes making
A strange noise
Knife scraping

Against glass
Sleeping in the back
Seat where

The money was
Laid out for the
Cops to find

If they had decided
To search the car
That night

Scent Of A Woman (The Musical)
Album Track Order

1. Hooha
2. Blind Drivin' & Hooha Hollerin'
3. My Balls, Your Face, Hooha!
4. Room Service Ice Cream
5. 100% Out Of 1000% Percent (My Ol' Blind Dick)
6. Dressing My Own Turkey
7. The One That Got Away
8. Deez Nutz
9. Coronas And Cabbage
10. Don't Go Breaking My Balls (Hooha Reprise)
11. Tony M's Lil' Sis' (She Ain't As Young As She Used To Be)
12. Evita: The Musical - A Ken Burns Documentary (The Song)
13. The Sugar Business
14. Tarantula

Ghosts

In the Home Depot
I hear the dead woman's voice
Singing 'We've only just begun'

She had stopped eating until
Her body ate her heart
And then she was dead and

Burned or buried
Her brother,
Left on earth

To grow older and mourn
Like the rest of us

If she were the only one
I might be able to handle it but
There are so many dead people

And I forget who's alive and who isn't
At this point, does it matter?
We're all lost to forever

Before too long

The Standard Apocalyptic 'That's The Way
We Do's It.' We All Gon' Die' But We Acting
Like It's All A'ight, Dick Poem

Most of the penises in the world
Are kept stashed away. Most of the time
Smooshed up inside underwear
Hidden away in pants or under skirts
Behind robes and sheets until it's time
To make some decisions or take a picture
And send it to someone's daughter
Or mother or an orphan even. One of
My best friends is an orphan, but she's older
Now.

I grew up in Germany where you see a
Lot more penis throughout the day
You can walk through the park and they're there
I saw my mom and dad's dick almost every day
Growing up. Even when we were a little older,
Like in our thirties and forties
My dad didn't mind being naked
Around us or our new families and
Friends

My dad misses the toilet a lot when he pees
And I've been doing it more and more I guess
I wouldn't have noticed but my wife has
Gotten on me about it. It's a rather sure
Sign that death is getting nearer
It'll knock on my door and take me back to
Another god and that'll be that
It's best to not think about it too often though,
Right?

The Hurdler

I was in a car commercial once
Portraying a housewife

Pretending to be a hobo
Riding a train across the country

My actor husband
Banished from heaven

Had bones growing into his eyes and
Sometimes at night I'd hear him

Crying quietly in his sleep

Spoon

When you spoon your ear
You'll hear the sun come out
Tomorrow

The lion doesn't use a spoon
When it eats its young
It forgoes the spoon

It was a full spoon
There was plenty to go around
But you weren't interested

I slept until everyone had gone to work
The werewolf has no place to put a spoon
And often buys replacement spoons

If you were to give me a spoon
Even a silver spoon
I'd still prefer a car

How many spoons does the ocean
Hide in its black belly
Under the cruel world of the living

I lied to you the way liars do
Because telling the truth was harder
Than trying to pass through the eye of a spoon

You lying there, spoon-like
And me wanting you to want me
With the moonlight eating away at the darkness

I took my spoon out of my pants and
Placed it on the desktop and

You gave me your opinion

When I was in France back in the 80's
I saw a stranger's spoon and I was struck
By how similar it was to my own

Maybe I Could Be Happy

He thought
Drinking the tap water
Alone in his kitchen

Wearing his
'I became a lesbian'
T-shirt and staring out

The window

Standing in his apartment
Somewhere on top of the earth
Where everything is

Surrounded by billions
Of stars in a space
Too vast to comprehend

The Bear

For a long time,
You don't even think about the bear
You walk through the forest without
A care in the world, listening to the radio
Discussing philosophy, wearing cologne

At some point that starts to change
You keep a gun in your bedside table
Keep your head on a swivel
Buy property near the beach
Hire people to sweat the small stuff

When it gets real dark
You start thinking that bear might
Not ever get around to showing up,
It'll let you sit there until you
Grow into a monster or worse

Don't worry though
The bear is on its way
With its magnificent hunger
It knows where you live
And has a copy of all your keys

I'll Leave It Up To You

Oak tree oak tree
Green and brown
With your feet in the air
And your head in the ground

Dead men dead men
The world floats away
Out into forever
Every single day

Your daddy's got a job
Working for the city
On the weekend
He's the president of the PTA

His hair's falling out
His mouth's all frown
The fireman's coming
To pull his teeth all out

Burn burn burn
In his SUV
But god is holding him
On his knee

Up in the heaven
Where all them people been
That you don't see in color
On your TV screen

Land Sharks

You can see their outlines
Dark shadows in the driveway
Just under the concrete

Waiting for you to fall in
Waiting for you to slip up
Waiting for you to get cocky

Oh, I knew they were there
I'd heard the stories
For years

I was hoping it was
Just some urban legend because
It hadn't been until recently

That I'd noticed their black curves
The slow still movement
Of their passing

Without Knowing Why

The lights had gone out.
The world was in darkness.
I could hear the animals
Making their beds
Beside me in the forest.

The lord was coming for us all.
It was better to not think about that
Or the day of reckoning that lay ahead
Instead we sang songs to keep
Our spirits up

But that was two years ago.

I'd almost forgotten about those
Desperate few hours we went without
Electricity until just this morning
When I sat down to write
This poem

Barney The Dinosaur
<How To Get Your Poetry Published>

I don't question it when you
Appear from out of inner space
In-between this world
And some other

<insert queer content>

Dazzling the eye
With blues and reds and greens
The children half-crazed
And calling your name

<insert rape event>

In what distant deeps or skies
Do you while away the hours
In what furnace is thy brain?
When you aren't breathing

<insert suicide of a sibling>

And the blood and bones
Become filler
And stitched cloth
And googly eyes

Shade Over Shade

They had become cartoons
Each with their finite cartoon hegemony
The weight of their eleven years together
Lighter than the leg of a sparrow

A carrier of fleas
A portrait of question marks
The reflection in the window
At night looking out into the abyss

The Liar

Hey kid with your wooden hands
Taking cookies out of the jar
Your father broke your head
Out of a tree

And now you are conversing
With insects? Sitting in the
Sun and dreaming
Of being a real person

One day you might be
Then you'll know
What true terror
Really is

The Town Where I Grew Up

If I was a robot
My hair would be brown
Or black depending
On how the light hit it

My lips would cover a
Mouth worn by a little
Boy too scared
To speak his mind

I'd sleep under a tiger
That died long ago
Only the bones
Would remain

I'd wear the
Shoes of a warrior
Modeled in the mirror
But never worn out

Into the world
With its wild outcomes
And inexplicable beauty

Millinery Row

Each one of your fingers
Wears a different hat
Depending on the day
And the specific event

For instance, your little finger
Will only wear a bonnet if
It won't stop raining and
The baby's in bed for the night

Your middle finger
Will wear a black bowler
Even on the hottest Saturday
Of the year

Your index finger will wear whatever
Hat you give her, but don't call
Her back into the hospital
No, it's better to call her Beatrice

Your ring finger will only wear a cowl
Along with a dark matching veil
I guess there is some history
Between it and your thumb

A bit of youthful adventure
That went badly and
Now separated only by time and
A few lonely inches
Is too much to bear

Other People's Gardens

If you want me to do something unpleasant like,
-the dishes
-sweep the floor
-ask for help
-go to bed at a reasonable hour
-brush my teeth
-take care of myself
-not question everything
-be nice to people who are boring
-stop buying stuff
-stop eating everything, all the time
-feed the plants
-walk the dog
-interact with my children
-wear something besides black
-say something non-critical
-be compassionate towards people who make
foolish decisions that will not only effect their lives
but your life and the life of your children as well
-go to a social gathering every once in a while. You
know, the usual sort of unpleasant stuff that the
road of life seems to be littered with

If that's what you want me to do
Just give me the choice between that
And having a feeling. Any kind of feeling

Down On The Drag

Before long
Nothing looks right
The tree across the street
Is walking towards me
In slow motion pulling out a gun
There's a small pig on the hood of a car
A cluster of children. Wait, those
Aren't children. Those are just some bushes
That look like children

And the tree holding that gun?
That's definitely my cousin Tom
His skin the consistency of buttermilk
His smile the color of Jesus

Spoiler Alert: It's Not Jesus

Who is that standing
At your shoulder
In that picture there

When you were seven
In your father's
Garden in your

Haircut and your
Powder blue pants
Your sister scowling

The world faded
Or the one where
You are standing on

The mountain
The whole world
Spread out below you?

Who is that there
At your wedding, and then at
Your son's first day of school

Just to your right
Beside you as the doctor
Sets the bone and

Makes it straight again
Or the picture you
Took just last night

In the living room
Of your friend's house

Just there in the

Corner waiting
So patiently for
The party to end

Let's Dance

The world is mostly ghosts
The ghost of the Vietnamese
Man getting shot by the ghost
Of the man shooting him
While another ghost watches on

All reviewing their roles in heaven now
Hitler. All the folks he murdered.
Stalin. All the folks he murdered.
Genghis Khan and whoever he raped or Killed
Everyone is at the after party celebrating and
Dancing and singing the old songs

Jesus Christ haranguing Pontius Pilate
Going on and on about how hard it was to
Die up on that stupid cross
'The role of a lifetime!' Pontius will respond

Suddenly David bowie is in the room
Pleading with me to put on
My red shoes and dance
Yes, I whisper, 'Let's dance",
Until we too are just memories

The Days I Have Left On This Earth

I see my daughter
Bend over and pick
Up something she dropped

And suddenly see the old
Cleaning lady who
Worked at the school

When I was a kid
And I think to myself that she
Was once a young little girl

Like my daughter
And at some point
Grew old and unlovable

And ended up living alone
And all the other things
That old ladies who's

Daddy's are dead
and buried in the ground
and who's name

You don't know
Or want to know
Do with what's left of their lives

Scarlet

I can't raise my spoon
My arms are too heavy
They weigh more than this
House

This house on the other
Hand is lighter than
Sunshine and floats
Through the air
Like the seasons of your heart

Birds keep feeding me
Feathers until I'm filled
With feathers and rise out
Of bed wringing the blood from my hair
Covering the walls of the bathroom

The morning dripping down
Into the sink where the
Baby is being washed
Away into forever one
Day at a time

The Eucharist

He took a rock and
Gave it to his disciples
And said, " This is my Thunderstone.
I won't need it where I'm going"
Dribbling wine onto his
Beautifully oiled beard

His disciples asked,
"Where art thou going Oh Lord?"
And the Lord said, "On up to
Haifa on the coast to relax
And get my shit together.
I've heard they've got some
Crazy little women there and
I'm a gonna get me one."

Of course he said
All of this in Aramaic
So who knows
What he really said.
Let's just say it's open
To interpretation

Walking Through The Dark Singing

How long does it take to write a poem?
Well, how long does it take to undress
And poop into the mouth of the great
River that runs through Ohio and then
Continues into the sea, where monsters
Live and die in the great darkness?
How long does it take to start the fire
That destroyed most of California back in the 70's?
How long does it take to cut off your hand
And immediately regret doing so?
Stuck now with only one hand
Unless this is your second time
Down this horrible fucking road
Maybe the first time wasn't the last time
Maybe the last time will be today
Handless. with no way to write a poem
Unless you use Siri, but that's going to be a real
Plane in the grass

And If It Happens

I guess I'll never be the musical guest on Saturday
Night Live and hang out with the cast at the end of
the show. Looking uncomfortable and not
enjoying myself and feeling bad that I can't seem
to have a good time. I'll never feel like I'm on top
of the world, having achieved this great level of
success, but not enjoying any of it. I'll never not be
making plans to hang out with the stars of the
show or make friends with anyone there,
pretending to not be intimidated by everyone and
thinking myself inferior to all of them. Hearing
their compliments, but not believing anything
they say, aware of how narcissistic and damaged
they all are and how much they want me to love
them as much as I need them to love me even
though I know it won't make a difference and I'll
never go back to my hotel room after the show and
be so glad that the night is over and that I made it
through the whole experience alive and now what
the fuck do I do with myself.

San Marcos

I threw out my voice
As far as I could
Calling you back
From where you'd gone

Beyond the lights
Where bears grow teeth
Alone in the forest
Surrounded by wolves

The Golden Treasury Of Knowledge

He took his robe and laid
It across his body and ran from
The room holding an old cell phone
From the 80's.

Singing the way they did
In the old country sang
Before telephones and
Global positioning systems.

Before the long war in the States
Before the end of the great British Baking Show
Before you began that cooking class
And made those amazing chicken fingers.
Before Gina and her girlfriend got together

Back when you could still confuse an audience
With talk of an afterlife and they'd peel off
Twenties and lay 'em on ya' until you could
Stack all that paper up to the ceiling.
Oh, what a wonderful feeling.

Ich Bin Der Manager

I opened a Guitar Center™ in Berlin
Almost five years ago. I'm the manager.
At the opening day ceremony
I burned a copy of Mother Theresa's
Autobiography because...Berlin

After my girlfriend moved out
I'd sit in the living room
With the lights off at night staring
At the television

Once, when the light had turned red
I drove through the intersection
The cars blurring past me on both sides
'You Take My Breath Away' blasting
Through the car speakers

"Try squeezing your feet into this"
She said once, while we were lying around
She was holding her old weather beaten
Copy of Mother Theresa's celebrated
Book where she sheds light on her
Self-serving life strategies

And The Oscar For Best Screenplay In The Category Of Everything Is...God

I sat down with god recently
For an interview and discussed
His latest Oscar win for best screenplay
Of everything.

BS: Thanks for joining us today

God: You're welcome

BS: So, one of the things that you came up with was the crucifixion of your son at the hands of the Romans. What made you come up with that idea?

God: Well, I'd already written crucifixion into the universal narrative and it was a pretty popular way to execute folks at the time. You must take into consideration that I hadn't created Ipads, Candy Crush™ or even moving pictures at that point, so there weren't a lot of entertainment options for people at that time other than the usually sorts of things people did, like rape, dance, and kill each other, and people really seemed to enjoy watching someone suffer in agony in public over the course of a couple of days. It really took the edge off the otherwise mundane existence of those times, and I thought what better way to create a memorable scene than to put my own son up on one of those crosses. Anyway, it worked like a charm. Plus, I'd written the part of my son as well, so I knew he'd be up for it no matter what. I'm very pleased at how big of a hit the crucifixion has been over the last two thousand years. Of course, that's also something I scripted, and, you know, not to get too meta, but I've even scripted this interview, so it's all pretty boring for me, like playing chess against myself. The only relief I get really, is to come to earth and forget who I am for a while and not have all the answers...You know, live a little!

A Funny Thing To Say

It was 1969
I was my daughter's age
I don't remember anything
Other than the sky opening up
And the whole world being
Swallowed by giants

It's Cool Being Young In The USA

If only you knew where you stood
In a room full of blood
Sure, the tigers are sleeping now
But not for much longer

A Turning Storm

When the Elvis became a lice
His visions intensified. There was
The one about the disfigured waitress
Drinking the blood of the mountain

When the Elvis shot dice
Behind his house out in the woods
He always carried a pistol in each hand
The wolves watching from the darkness

When the rains came
For a hundred years
There were no more streets
No one to return your calls

Just the slow hard longing
The wild feeling that lasted
A hundred million or more years
Where not a word was spoken

*Mr Fantastic Brand Everything Rainbow
Wonderhead And My Mouth Won't Stop
Smiling Now That The New Day Has Opened
Up Its Head Announcing Your Place In The
World And The Sunshine Is Brighter Than
Laser Sugar*

Everything is green and pink
And orange and not black or grey
My arms are connected to my body
And so are my fingers

I'm not shot in the head
Or lying in a pool of acid in
A basement behind a factory
Or waiting to be burned by an angry mob

All of my wives are happy
And so are my fourteen goats
And also my chickens and all my crops
Are ready to be eaten by bugs

No one has more hands than me
I've got two, at least for now
When everything is going just right
Even though I'm being told right now

That there are some serious problems
That need to be addressed
Right after this quick commercial
Break from our sponsors

He Had The Best Hair At The Table

They called him
Dr. Hair

Occasionally

In Her Bed

Every once in a while
You get in the zone

You see clearly how limitless
The possibilities are

Of course then,
There are days like this

What the fuck Po Poo?

Where and why Po Poo?
In the morning
Under clear days of gold?
When we swam in our robes or
Laying clothed on the shores
Of the Roman beaches?

Your hair looking pretty good
The sun falling into your skin
Pouring beer onto the beach
While the biker's booed

I want more of that
But you can't swim backwards
Against the currents of time
They'll drag you out into the dessert
They'll build a fire out of bricks

All The Chocolate You Can Swirl

OK...repeat the line:
'Why can't we be friends' over and over
Then buy a new car with all that money
and marry a stranger
Then have kids (maybe) and get
divorced and get old and die
(But not yet-listen to me when I'm talking)

Are you working for the CIA?
I feel like you might be, because
I'm pretty sure you're not working for the mafia
(pronounced Mah-Fah-Yay!)
Did you see 'Dragged Across Concrete' yet?
It's pretty good.
Not as good as that guys other two movies,
but pretty good.

The Way They Were

The little boy bug left for the day
And died in my toilet
I wonder if his mother
Worried after him

Did she imagine that
He had found a new beginning
Somewhere. Perhaps
Made some startling new discovery

What alien thoughts
Might be going through
Her mind when he didn't
Return from that day's adventures

Sitting there on the couch
Enjoying a beverage, another episode
Of the Bachelorette or
Being eaten by a great bird

One Dead Guy Showing Another Dead Guy What's What

I was reading Raymond Carver's
Book of poems this morning, and got to
The one about him meeting
Charles Bukowski at some party

He just wrote down
Some of the things
He recalled Bukowski saying,
And it exposed how simple and easy

The thing that Bukowski does is
If you're Raymond Carver,
That is

Through The Doorway

There was a sound
Coming from the kitchen
Above the stove
Maybe

Something alive
Looking for a way out
Or in. I can't be sure
Anymore

When Asked My Religion

I searched the woods for a wolf and found
Your grandmother making soup
Hansel had become a lawyer
Suffering horribly from PTSD

Gretel never made it through high school
They found her hanging from
A skylight in the girls locker room
She'd become a robot again

Spelling everything in German
Unlocking the gun case
Twisting the cork out
And ruining her dress

I took down the chisel
From the christmas tree
Peeling the scars off my arms
Pooling the secretary team

Does It Make For A Better Story?

When you describe the
Condemned man atop the gallows
Looking through the hangman's noose
Contemplating his eminent demise
Or you see him standing in the shower
Staring at the last few bites of his candy bar

Laughing On (the inside) Leadenly

Everything was
Just a joke to him
He had such a hard time
Taking anything seriously

He was once quoted as saying,
'We have given our hearts away'
In a moving speech about the
1860 presidential election

But then he followed it
Up with a whole slew
Of dick jokes that made the entire
Assembly uncomfortable

After a time he died
And people eventually
Forgot about him and
That was that

A Young Man On A Horse

A young man on a horse
Taking his medication
His pants are in the oven
The fish are in the street

A young man on a horse
He's robbing the neighbors
There's a reason for everything
He tells his daughters tucking them in

A young man on a horse
His hands trembling in the sun
The cold sores disappearing
He's making his own bed now

A young man on a horse
There's no reason to have a liver
What sort of god makes livers
And spleens if we're really going to get into it

A young man on a horse
The fact that there are livers
Is one of the few reasons left
To not believe in a loving and giving god

A young man on a horse
Covered in bee bites
The reins resting by his feet
His dreams lost in the trees

To Sing

And then,
And then,
And then,

Nothing